AN INTRODUCTION TO LACE

Fig. 1
Rare and valuable Hollie-point sampler, 1732

Gabrielle Pond

An Introduction To Lace

CHARLES SCRIBNER'S SONS
New York

1 3 5 7 9 11 13 15 17 19 MD/C 20 18 16 14 12 10 8 6 4 2

Printed in the United States of America
Library of Congress Catalog Card Number 75-7882
ISBN 0-684-13830-1

CONTENTS

ILLUSTRATIONS

viii

"Greek, Sir, is like lace; every man gets as much of it as he can."

Dr Samuel Johnson, 1780

FOREWORD

During the last fifty years interest in hand-made lace, and the knowledge of it, steadily declined. So general was this lack of interest that unwanted pieces have been consigned to the dustbin although they might be over two hundred years old and have cost as much as £300 a yard at the time they were made. *The Tablet of Memory*, London, 1787, said that lace was ". . . more valuable than gold. One ounce of fine Flanders thread has been sold in London for £1. Such an ounce made into lace may here be sold for £40, which is ten times the price of standard gold, weight for weight."

In the five years since the first edition (much smaller and in paper covers) of this book the mounting interest in bygones has begun to extend to lace.

There are now new books appearing, as well as reprints of old ones. Classes for making bobbin lace are available in most districts and fully booked. Both lace and bobbins are eagerly sought in shops, markets and family hoards. Good 18th century pieces now fetch highly competitive prices at auction, and lace is no longer thrown away without an effort being made to ascertain whether any of it is saleable.

There are nowadays few examples of any skilled craftsmanship from the past which are not eagerly sought by collectors, and the law of supply and demand makes for rapidly increasing prices and the production of fakes, yet lace is one of the few antiques which is under-valued and cannot be faked. Neither the fine flax thread from which antique lace was made, nor the necessary skill to make use of its quality, will ever be available again and, if they were, it would not be economically worthwhile to attempt to imitate—although some lace is still made in England and elsewhere and good machine-made copies have been manufactured for well over a hundred years.

Antique dealers cannot be specialists in everything, and as lace for many years had no market value they naturally do not trouble to learn about it nor to stock it.

11

This places the collector in a strong position because, although lace is hard to find, it may cost little or nothing. As I write, however, there are definite signs of awakening interest. Owners naturally hesitate to throw away something which has been greatly cherished by previous generations and are often glad to find a good home for it. Unless homes are found, and the lace kept in good condition, all the wonderful collections in private hands will eventually disappear.

The subject is an intricate one which requires deep and careful study to reach full appreciation, but there is nevertheless much of general interest for those who desire only to know enough of the history and technique of lace-making to be able to enjoy its beauty. To provide such information is the purpose of this book, which covers the first approach to looking at lace, how to date it and how to conserve it. Some of the suggestions as to its care and use deviate from the advice given in older books, but all are the result of personal experience. A real understanding can only be acquired by reading books, studying collections and handling as many pieces as possible. There are a number of lace-making schools in London and other parts of the country, and to learn the craft is even better. Older ladies, who still treasure their laces, will usually lend them for study, and books on lace can be found in second-hand bookshops and public libraries.

There is, thankfully, only one expenditure essential to the study of lace and that is a magnifying glass, preferably with a diameter of not less than two inches and × 5 magnification.

Finally I must say that I am indebted to Mrs Alison Adburgham for information about lacemen from *Shops and Shopping, 1800–1914* (George Allen and Unwin), to the City of Liverpool Museums for photographs from their collections, to Ash Design for Figs. 1, 2, 3, 14, 17, 23, 24, 27–33 and 36–38, and to the late Miss E. L. Eveleth of The International Old Lacers of America for the benefit of her wisdom and experience.

Gabrielle Pond

1

THE HISTORY OF LACE

Some form of mesh or network has been discovered in ancient Egyptian tombs and since then forms of embroidery approximating to lace have been made in all ages throughout the Middle East, whence the craft travelled via Italy all over Europe. It is not possible to say at exactly what date lace, as we think of it, was first made, but it is known that lace made by bobbin and by needle existed before the 16th century in Italy and the Low Countries. The kinds of lace made in mediaeval times were mostly fine cutwork, drawn-thread and darned netting, called Lacis. Crochet was also made from a very early date, especially in nunneries.

From the 16th century both needle and bobbin lace also feature in portraits and records, and the stiff ruffs of Tudor times were edged with a needle-lace known as Reticella.

Early in the 17th century, ruffs and high Medici collars went out of fashion and the soft falling collars, such as are seen in Van Dyck's portraits of Charles I and his family, were worn instead. Lace became heavier, richer, wider and increasingly beautiful. The skill shown in the large decorative pieces made during this period is unbelievable. Portraits of the period show very well how the lace was displayed and the immense quantities worn by both men and women. Samuel Pepys speaks of "my Lady Castlemaine's underwear, all trimmed with fine lace, blowing in the wind" at St. James's Palace. At first the best lace was made in Italy and Flanders, but about 1665 Louis XIV founded lace schools in France under the tuition of Venetian experts, and very fine lace was also made during this period in England. Most European countries also had their own lace centres, though their quality was generally not so high. Gold and silver lace was made chiefly by the Jews in Spain, though the craft was spread when they were expelled to other countries.

Lace continued to be highly prized during the 18th century, and very highly priced. The manufacture was slow and laborious and supply never equalled demand. This led to a vast amount of smuggling between one country and another and there are many curious tales of the subterfuges used to avoid the heavy excise duties imposed. Smuggled lace was as much trouble to the excise man as brandy! Under the cover of a false fur overcoat it was wrapped round dogs, which were turned loose to find their way home across the frontier between Flanders and France. It was concealed in every way ingenuity could devise, even in coffins containing real corpses. When discovered, the lace was impounded or burnt and very heavy penalties were imposed.

Towards the end of the century, however, the first signs of decline appeared. The most important factor was the French Revolution in 1789. Not only did the lace centres and workers all over France suffer violence and even death at the hands of the rabble, associated as they were with the extravagant tastes of the aristocracy, but the complete change of fashion in dress to the severe and simple lines of the Directoire style brought the whole industry almost to extinction. Early in the 19th century, when Napoleon I ordered an elaborate layette for the infant King of Rome, there was great difficulty in finding enough surviving lacemakers to carry out the royal commands.

Later, in the 19th century, many philanthropic women made attempts to revive the industry in Europe, but their efforts were only moderately successful owing to the progress already being made in the manufacture of machine-made lace. Net had been made by machine in the first decade of the century and as early as 1837, the first year of Queen Victoria's reign, the wife of the American Ambassador to

14

Britain was given by Nottingham manufacturers a court dress of machine-made lace of which she was extremely proud. However, in spite of difficulties, enough lace-makers were trained to keep the industry alive, and towards the end of the century fine laces were again being made in some quantity in Italy and Belgium. During the later years of the 19th century lace was still an essential part of a lady's attire and was often given as a present. Antique pieces were greatly sought after and treated with the utmost care, and it was a test of a good dressmaker or lady's maid that she should know how to manipulate lace elegantly without cutting or damaging it. It is difficult to realise the immense value placed on lace, not only financially but as a status symbol. In *Madame Giovanni* Alexandre Dumas writes describing a hotel fire in California: "The alarm sounding, Mrs Plum ran to the box that held her money, jewels and laces."

The queens of England have always been great patrons of the lace industry. Mary II, wife of William of Orange, was herself skilled in the craft, probably learned in the Low Countries before her accession, and she even worked during long and bumpy coach journeys. Queen Anne's favourite lace was the soft and dainty Mechlin (Malines) which she used lavishly. Queen Charlotte, wife of George III, preferred Brussels lace, which was always worn at court. Adelaide, Queen of William IV, had a wedding dress specially made of Honiton lace to encourage home industry, and Honiton was also used for the wedding dresses of Queen Victoria, Queen Alexandra and Queen Mary in more recent times. The royal babies are still christened in a beautiful Honiton robe. Queen Victoria wore a great deal of fine lace during her long reign, and on her death her collection was valued at £76,000. There is a remarkable lace dress still extant in Switzerland which was made for the Empress Eugenie about 1855 during the fashion for the huge crinoline. Thirty-six workers were employed on it for eighteen months and it has been estimated that had it been made by a single pair of hands it would have taken thirty years to complete.

Up to the end of the century very fine pieces of English

and Irish lace were specially made for exhibitions, and smaller pieces for general use. No effort, however, to popularise the industry could compete with the rapid improvement in machine-made lace. By the end of the 19th century lace-making as an industry had almost died out.

2

THE DECLINE OF LACE FROM 1900

Much has been written on the subject of lace up to the early years of the 20th century, when it was still collected, admired, highly-priced and worn with pride and elegance. Even at that time it was still being smuggled in quantity, owing to the high duty on lace made abroad. It is interesting to consider the total decline of value and interest which took place in the short space of the following thirty years.

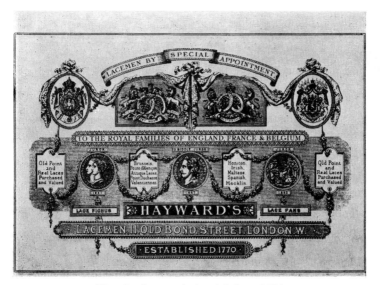

Fig. 2   Laceman's box label, c. 1870.

It is interesting to note that lacemen—retailers who made their living solely by selling hand-made lace—existed in great numbers in all large cities from the 17th century onwards. Lace was used for personal adornment on all occasions—the officers of the Earl of Argyll's regiment lined up before the battle of Glencoe wearing their lace cravats. It was widely used for church decoration and vestments and among the wealthy people for household linen and even servants' clothes. The royal coaches were lined with lace.

The demand always exceeded the supply, orders took a long time to fulfil and prices were unbelieveably high. It was not unusual for a single piece of lace to cost thousands of pounds. Naturally the best pieces were most carefully handled and were passed down as heirlooms from one generation to another for over two hundred years, each generation adding new treasures as older ones wore out.

As wealth increased in the 19th century, so did the number of people who could afford rich personal adornment. Although the number of lace workers was steadily decreasing, owing to the increase of machine-made lace and the opportunities of better-paid work, the lacemen increased in number, as did the volume of business. However, the quality of lace gradually deteriorated. In 1817 there were five lacemen in Oxford Street alone, then only on the verge of the main shopping district of London, but by the middle of the century some of these had moved into department stores, of which the largest floor space was given over to lace. In 1867 the third largest turnover from Whiteley's seventeen departments was from the sale of lace, and amounted to £3,500. In 1895 Peter Robinson's lace department sold a total of £25,958 worth. These departments would undoubtedly have included household and machine-lace as well as hand-made, but in the early years of the 20th century there were still many establishments trading only in the best quality hand-made and antique laces suitable for weddings, christenings and court occasions, as well as to tempt collectors.

Dress in the Edwardian period tended to be vastly over-trimmed, with ribbons, frills, braid and feathers as well as lace. Good lace was no longer obtainable in large enough quantities to cover the demand and although plenty of the less expensive Irish lace, such as crochet and embroidered net, was still made, the majority of dressmakers had to be content with machine-made imitations, and the best family pieces were used only for special occasions. Little girls, like their mamas, had their petticoats and drawers lavishly frilled with lace, and whether it was "real" or not was a great source of rivalry among old-fashioned nannies. Collectors were still buying antique pieces at high prices as an investment and lengths of fine quality were often given for wedding or christening presents. It is interesting to know that Fred Terry and Julia Neilson were not only collectors but always insisted on wearing real, contemporary lace for *The Scarlet Pimpernel* and other costume plays.

The 1914 war threatened to end the manufacture and use of hand-made lace just as the French Revolution in 1789 had threatened the craft in its time. The lace industry in Belgium was only kept going with the help of a committee of American ladies who organised the supplies of materials necessary for the workers and also the marketing of their wares abroad. After the war there were more than enough better-paid jobs for the few remaining lace workers and, as had happened before, fashions changed suddenly to clothes which were simple, practical and comparatively unadorned. The generation which grew up during the war had no use for the frumpish trimmings which looked so odd in old family photographs.

Machine-made lace was still used as a material for dresses and applied to underwear in modest quantities, but "real" lace had become, by this time, irreplaceable, and was considered by the older generation to be too frail and valuable to be cut and used in this way. Hand-made lace disappeared from the counters of department stores, and in the twenties only two or three lacemen remained in London's West End to provide fine trimmings for baby-

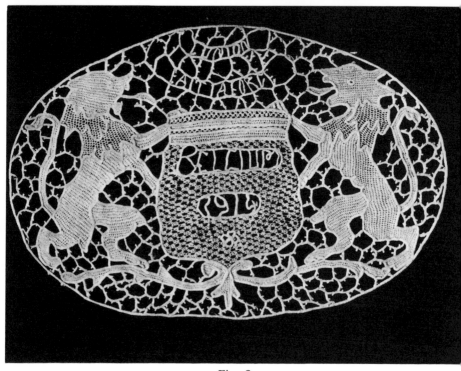

Fig. 3
Needlepoint panel made in Belgium during the 1914–18 War,
under the auspices of the Red Cross, for the British and
American markets.

clothes and trousseaux and rare specimens for the few
remaining collectors.

The slump years of the early thirties had their effect on
all luxury trades and from this time on we hear no more of
"real" lace or lacemen. It was already nearly twenty years
since the wearing of good lace had ceased to be fashionable
and the new generation only thought of it, if at all, as the
lowest form of dowdiness. It was put away and forgotten,
carefully wrapped in mauve or black tissue-paper, often in
specially made boxes. On the death of its owner it was
stored away with other junk, retained only from sentiment
and a lingering tradition of its being very valuable.

By the time another war had come and gone, houses
had less room for storing unnecessary boxes and few people

20

remained who knew or cared anything about lace. It had not been a saleable commodity for more than a generation and dealers were not interested. In consequence it was frequently thrown away, or even burnt, as having no value at all.

During the recent years of inflationary advances in the price of anything old or hand-made, it is astonishing that the position of lace remains so much the same. Few books have been published on the subject in the last fifty years, and lace is still completely outside the knowledge of most antique dealers.

There is, however, a new consciousness of the beauty and craftsmanship of old pieces and people do try to find out something about their family heirlooms before deciding to consign them to the dustbin. There is also a considerable revival in the craft of bobbin lace-making, and tuition is available in most districts. In America there is an international society of "Old Lacers", and there are a number of lace societies in England and Wales. Also there has recently been a very noticeable improvement in prices given for 18th century lace and it might therefore seem that lace is coming into its own again.

3

SORTING AND IDENTIFICATION

Though many large and elaborate old pieces can be seen in our museums and art galleries, the pieces most likely to come into private possession are either wedding veils and flounces or smaller pieces such as collars, caps and lappets, handkerchiefs, fans, baby clothes or edging from half to six inches deep. There is great satisfaction in being able to tell when, where and how these pieces were made, but these questions can only be answered after diligent study. It is necessary to determine whether it is hand-made or machine-made, what kind of lace it is, where it was made, how old it is and also if it is a piece of exceptional quality. Can it be cleaned and mended, and are there any uses for it? Surprisingly, the most difficult question to answer may be the first—hand-made or machine-made? Let us, however, first consider what type of lace it is. It may be bobbin lace, needlepoint lace or one of a type which can be classified as embroidery lace. It is of great importance to understand the differing nature of these types. Bobbin and needle-lace are used as the basis of many different types of lace, either worked inch by inch along the length of the piece, or in sprigs which may be joined by mesh background or bridges into a complete design, or mounted on net.

BOBBIN LACE. The method employed with bobbin lace is plaiting and weaving threads wound on to bobbins. The lace is made on a firm pillow to which a pricked-out pattern is tacked and each twist of the bobbins is held in place by a pin. The pattern is formed by more compact weaving than that used in making the mesh, the whole being enlivened by a variety of filling. The design is some-

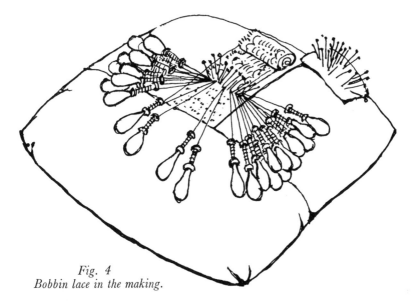

Fig. 4
Bobbin lace in the making.

times outlined in a heavier thread. Almost all English laces were originally copied from the laces made at Valenciennes, Lille, Mechlin and Brussels, all of which have individual characteristics of réseau and toile. A simple type of bobbin lace was introduced into England by Katherine of Aragon and is still made in the Midlands and other schools of lace-making. Though nowadays generally classed as Torchon it was, in the 19th century, still referred to as Katherine of Aragon lace. Bobbin lace is sometimes referred to as pillow lace, although other types of lace were also made on a pillow.

Until the middle of the last century, lace was woven from the finest flax thread, which was made in Belgium, and the work was so skilled that the spinners received comparatively high wages. The thread is so fine that it cannot be felt between the finger and thumb. That used for the best laces was so delicate that both spinning and lace-making had to be done in a damp cellar to prevent the thread from becoming brittle, thus avoiding constant breaks. Usually four workers sat round a small table on which stood a glass globe of water between each of them and the single candle in the middle. These globes acted as lenses which concentrated the light into a beam which lit up a small part of the work on the pillow. How the workers could see, by this illumination, to produce such beautiful work is almost incomprehensible! It is no wonder that a worker's eyesight often failed by the age of thirty. Lace was sometimes made in the loft above the cowhouse, where the workers could get some warmth in the winter without smoke and dirt from the fires. Moreover, it was a very slow process. Fine pieces of medium width could only be made at the rate of a few inches per day; unusually wide ones might take a whole day to get across the pattern and would employ as many as a thousand bobbins. Even a border less than an inch across might require up to eighty bobbins, depending on the pattern.

Children of both sexes were taught the craft from the age of three, first learning to wind the bobbins and then to make the narrow footings. Though most of the lace workers were women, there were also men workers as late as the middle of the 19th century. At this time children worked four to five hours per day and adults up to fifteen hours, though even the most skilled could not earn more than sixpence a day.

Sailors spent spare time ashore and afloat on lacemaking. (Did not Lewis Carrol, in *The Hunting of the Snark*, immortalise ". . . the beaver who sat making lace in the bows"?) In 1851 there were still nearly five hundred thousand lace workers in Europe, half of whom were in France. Nevertheless, when it came to the making of Queen Victoria's wedding gown, which cost £1,000, it was difficult to find sufficient workers in Devonshire.

Here are some of the best known bobbin laces:

Point d'Angleterre *(see Figs. 5, 6)*. Experts disagree as to the origin of this lace. Mrs Nevill Jackson in her book *(A History of Hand Made Lace,* published in 1900) gives excellent reasons for believing that it originated in England and was imitated in Flanders for the English market. Other authorities maintain that it was only made in Flanders, so its origin remains in dispute. It was made between 1650 and 1750, and the workmanship is so fine and the designs of such beauty that it cannot possibly be appreciated by the naked eye. It differs from other contemporary Flemish lace chiefly in having loose threads carried across the back of the leaves and flowers.

Honiton *(see Figs. 7, 8, 9)*. Very fine lace was made in many

Fig. 5
Point d'Angleterre Brussels lace lappets; early 18th century.

places in Devonshire from the 17th century, but of these Honiton is the best known. The sprigs and motifs were worked separately and then arranged in a pattern and either joined by bobbin réseau or bridges, or sewn on net. Honiton lace was extensively used during the Victorian era, but by the second half of the 19th century the traditional patterns had become debased and hardly recognisable as the earlier floral sprays.

Fig. 6
Enlargement of right-hand lappet in Fig. 5.

Fig. 7
Fan made in 1889 with Honiton lace.

Fig. 8
Honiton lace collar, c. 1870, and bow of East Midlands lace,
c. 1870.

Valenciennes *(see Figs. 10, 11, 32)*. Strong, usually narrow edging or insertion such as used on underwear or baby-clothes. Designs include dots, simple flowers and a scalloped edge, and mesh may be round or square. Lace of this type was made with designs of naturalistic flowers and older pieces have complicated, close réseau, with no cordonnet.

Binche. A Flemish bobbin lace with elaborate forms of mesh background. Old Binche has a flat, close weave with no cordonnet, similar to Valenciennes. Designs are usually flower sprays, but sometimes animals. 18th century examples of these two laces are especially soft and fine to touch.

Lille *(see Fig. 26)*. The réseau is round and clear. The designs of conventional flowers and scrolls are outlined in heavier thread and tend to be small and chiefly at the lower edge of the flounce.

Mechlin *(see Figs. 10, 29)*. Very fine and soft to touch, usually made with an intricate hexagonal mesh. The earlier designs were very elaborate and beautiful but later have a light design of dots and separate flowers outlined in a thicker thread, with a straight edge. Much used for a border for Indian muslins in the earlier years of the 19th century.

Brussels *(Figs. 5, 6, 10, 11, 13, 16)*. Old Brussels lace is of fine texture and rich in design, with a hexagonal mesh similar to Mechlin. It was often made, as with Honiton, in separate sprays sewn on net, which in the earlier days was hand-made and known as "vrai réseau" to distinguish it from the machine-made net, which was used from early in the 19th century. The sprays were also sometimes joined by hand-made réseau or by bars, which was a less laborious method and generally used for the coarser type of guipure much in demand at the end of the century.

Point de Milan *(see Fig. 27)*. A wide and handsome lace with réseau ground and flowing bold design with intricate fillings.

Maltese *(see Fig. 10)*. A guipure made of silk or cotton

thread. Geometrical designs often including a Maltese cross. Much favoured for collars and cuffs and shawls at the end of the 19th century. Usually of a deep cream colour owing to the discoloration of the silk thread, and sometimes black.

Fig. 9
(From left to right) East Midlands bobbin lace, c. 1870. Buckingham spider pattern bobbin lace, c. 1870. Honiton bobbin lace, c. 1870. Traditional Torchon Bedfordshire bobbin lace.

Fig. 10
(From left to right) Mechlin bobbin lace, early 19th century. Valenciennes bobbin lace, late 19th century. Brussels Duchesse lace, late 19th century. Traditional Maltese lace. Venetian Corraline bobbin lace.

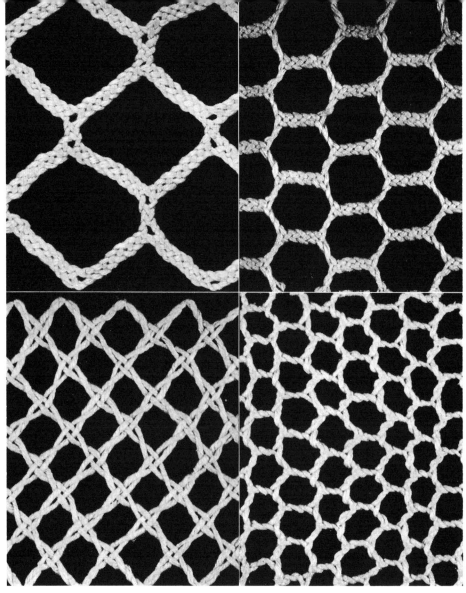

Fig. 11
(*Meshes: From left to right*) *Valenciennes—square or diamond mesh. Brussels—Droschel or Vrai Réseau mesh. Torchon— Other more elaborate meshes are also used. Alençon—Like Point de Gaze, but the loops are whipped over after each row is made.*

Buckinghamshire *(see Fig. 9)*. This resembles Lille lace with round réseau and pretty floral designs and fillings, the toile being outlined in heavier thread. It can be of any width, but it is usually rather narrow (from a half to four inches).

Other Midland Laces *(see Fig. 9)*. These were made in several centres including Bedfordshire and Nottinghamshire, but being much alike are difficult to identify with any certainty as belonging to a particular locality. Those made in the later part of the 19th century tend to be narrow and simple in design. Bedfordshire lace-makers often used Maltese and Torchon designs during this period.

Torchon *(see Figs. 9, 11)*. A common type of lace made chiefly in England and France from cotton or flax, in geometrical designs, rather similar to Maltese. It is often coarse and used principally for household linens.

NEEDLEPOINT. This type of lace evolved from embroidery on fine linen. The background material was at first cut away leaving open spaces which were filled or bridged with a variety of stitches. Later the linen base was discarded altogether and the whole fabric made by needle and thread in various forms of buttonhole-stitch. Like bobbin lace, it is made upon a pillow. The design is first outlined in one or two strands, which are lightly tacked to the parchment pattern. This is then filled in with close stitching and the background is made either by a réseau of looser stitches or by bridges, which may be ornamented with little stars or picots. Many lovely open fillings were designed to give a lighter and more varied effect. Needlepoint is very strong and often given extra strength by a thicker thread or cord oversewn to the outline of the toile. This work was extremely laborious but both beautiful and durable, and has always been highly prized. It is almost impossible to realise that every single stitch was made separately with a needle. There are a number of well-known needlepoint laces.

Reticella *(See Fig. 12)*. The earliest kind of needlepoint; a

Fig. 12
Reticella needlepoint collar, late 19th century.

close, geometrical form with a serrated edge.

Point de Venise *(See Figs. 13, 14)*. This is the most famous needlepoint of all and is bold, imaginative and flowery in design. The flowers are built up with raised edges, almost into low relief, and the sprays joined by elaborately looped bridges. The effect is almost like carved ivory. This lace was much worn in the 17th and 18th centuries. Excellent pieces were again made in Burano, Venice, at the end of the 19th century.

Point de France. A lace similar to Point de Venise, but the motifs are joined by hexagonal mesh.

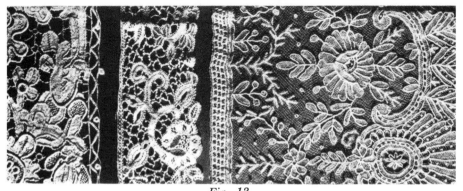

Fig. 13
(From left to right) Point de Venise needlepoint lace, middle 18th century. Irish needlepoint lace, middle 19th century. Brussels Point appliqué, c. 1880.

Fig. 14
Point de Venise needlepoint, early 18th century.

Point d'Alençon and Point d'Argentan *(see Fig. 15)*. These types of lace were made in France from about 1650 but later also in Venice at Burano. They have a lighter and more gauzy appearance as the réseau is made entirely of fine loose buttonholing, which gives the effect of clear net. The toile in Point d'Alençon is outlined with raised thread sometimes padded with horsehair, and the mesh of Argentan is often worked all over in buttonhole stitch, which makes it more solid.

Fig. 15
Detail of Point d'Alençon.

Point de Gaze *(see Fig. 16)*. This is a Brussels lace, much in demand in later Victorian times. The designs, as with all laces, follow the fashion. From the middle of the 19th century they show garlands and sprays of naturalistic flowers on a fine clear réseau. The flowers are often built up with layers of superimposed petals. Both this lace and Alençon were also made in Burano during the 19th century.

Hollie-Point *(see Figs. 1, 17)*. This is a lace of close texture with the design pricked out in tiny holes. It was made from the middle ages until the mid-18th century. Originally used for religious occasions, such as weddings and christenings (hence the name "holy point"), after the reformation it was also used for lay purposes.

34

Fig. 16
Fan made with Point de Gaze Brussels lace, 1860–80.

Fig. 17
Baby's cap trimmed with Hollie-point and edged with Old Valenciennes, mid-18th century.

Irish Point *(see Fig. 13)*. Made in Ireland in the mid-19th century in imitation of Venetian-point designs, but the effect is more angular and less imaginative.

MIXED LACES COMBINING BOBBIN AND NEEDLE-POINT.

Duchesse *(see Fig. 10)*. A Belgian guipure of bobbin sprays which often has medallions of Point de Gaze. This lace was

Fig. 18
(From top to bottom) Italian Tape guipure, early 18th century. Brussels bobbin lace with needlepoint insertions, c. 1870.

very popular in the last two decades of the 19th century. Earlier, Brussels lace often shows bobbin motifs joined by needle ground.

Tape Lace *(see Fig. 18)*. A considerable amount was made in Italy, particularly in Milan and Turin. The design was formed from narrow bobbin-made tape, the fillings and réseau or bridges being of bobbin or needlepoint. Making "point lace" of this kind was a popular form of needlework among ladies of leisure in the last century, but the tape was machine-made and the results often clumsy and amateurish.

Fig. 19
(From left to right) Irish crochet handkerchief, 1900–20. Brussels mixed lace handkerchief, 1880–90. Carrickmacross handkerchief, 1870–80.

APPLIQUÉ. This simply means the application, by sewing, of one material to another. Although originally a base of hand-made réseau was used, it was very arduous work and from about 1806 the invention of machine net caused a great increase in appliqué. Wedding veils and flounces could be made with less than half the expenditure of time and money without seriously affecting the appearance of the work. Appliqué laces include the following:

Brussels *(see Fig. 13)*. Naturalistic sprays of bobbin or needle-lace or of fine net applied to net ground. In older specimens the net was sometimes cut away from behind the lace.

Honiton. Bobbin sprays on a net ground. This technique was widely used for wedding veils.

Carrickmacross *(see Figs. 19, 20)*. Most of this lace dates from about 1850. Fine cambric, muslin or net was tacked to a net ground and the outline of the pattern was embroidered through both materials. The unwanted superimposed fabric was then carefully cut away leaving an elegant design, of flowers and leaves.

CUTWORK. This is one of the earliest forms of lace known. It is a design embroidered in outline on fine cotton or linen and the individual motifs joined by bridges to complete the design. The background is then cut away. This type of lace was also made in Carrickmacross.

TAMBOUR. Another type of embroidered lace which consists of a design worked on machine net by needle or hook in fine chain stitch. This was also a pastime favoured by amateurs and when well done is elegant and pretty. At the end of the 19th century much Tambour lace was made by using a sewing-machine. Tambour lace includes the following:

Isle of Wight. *(see Fig. 28)*. A coarsely worked lace of simple design made during the latter half of the 19th century and favoured by Queen Victoria for her cap strings.

Fig. 20
(From top to bottom; all mid-Victorian) Carrickmacross scarf. Limerick Tambour handkerchief. Darned bonnet veil. Filet darning.

Brussels. Was made in this same way, usually with elaborate designs of flowers and scrolls.

Limerick *(see Fig. 20)*. Similar to Brussels, but the designs were generally simpler. The Irish harp and shamrock were sometimes included.

CROCHET *(see Figs. 19, 21, 22).* Crochet is an old-established craft, known to have been made in nunneries from the 15th century. The only lace of distinction in this category was made in Ireland, where its manufacture was encouraged by philanthropic ladies during the last century. At first it was merely copied from Italian designs but it soon developed a strongly national characteristic appearance. It is made with a fine crochet hook and cotton thread and the

Fig. 21
(From top to bottom; all late Victorian) Knitted lace collar.
Tatting. Irish crochet cap.

most familiar type is worked from a central rose or shamrock outwards to a square up to two inches in size. The individual squares are then invisibly joined to any required shape or size. It is still being made.

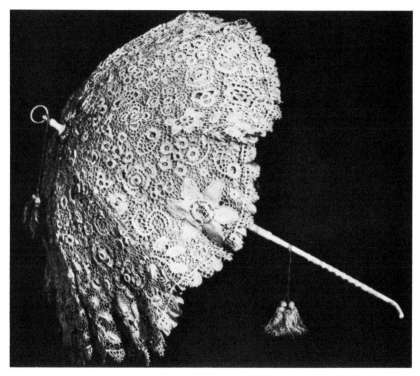

Fig. 22
Irish Crochet parasol, 1850–65.

DRAWN-THREAD WORK *(see Fig. 23)*. The threads of linen were not cut but pulled into groups with needle and thread. This was one of the earliest forms of open embroidery, brought to great perfection in the 18th century, especially in Denmark and Germany. It is known as Tönder lace or Dresden work.

Fig. 23
Drawn-thread work; Danish or Dresden. First half of 18th
century.

DARNED NETTING *(see Fig. 20)*. Machine net was also used as a background for embroidering a pattern with fine silk or flax thread. Much was made in Ireland, especially in Limerick. In Spain and Italy black or white silk thread was used.

FILET or **LACIS** *(see Fig. 20)*. Patterns darned on to a square-meshed hand-made netting. It is one of the earliest forms of lace known; now usually rather coarse and used for household linens and mainly made in France and Italy.

KNITTED LACE *(see Fig. 21)*. Lace made by knitting has never achieved any great degree of refinement. Pretty designs for edging household linen can be carried out in cotton thread, and some of the shawls made in Shetland wool are beautiful.

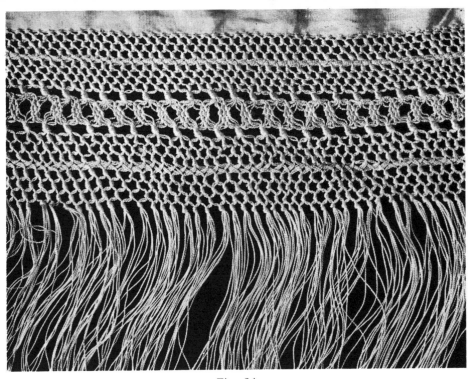

Fig. 24
Macramé fringe, modern.

MACRAMÉ *(see Fig. 24).* A fringe of silk, linen or cotton knotted into a design.

TATTING *(see Fig. 21).* This is a knotted lace of simple design, made with a cotton thread wound on a shuttle. It is still a universally popular handicraft.

BLACK LACE. Most collections include some black lace, as this was in great favour during the 19th century, when custom demanded that mourning should be worn for long periods, and it was even more popular in Latin countries than in England. Much of it is machine-made but may nevertheless well be over a hundred years old. Most lace-making centres produced black lace as well as white and many of the pieces will be of the types already mentioned including Bedfordshire, Torchon borders and shawls, and

43

mantillas of Maltese lace and darned silk net. Other types more frequently found in black than white include these:

Chantilly *(see Fig. 25)*. This is an old and beautiful lace which became almost extinct after the French Revolution but was revived by the middle of the 19th century. It is a

Fig. 25
Chantilly lace parasol, 1850–65.

bobbin lace made of dull silk thread with a delicate pattern of flower sprays upon a clear mesh ground, the design outlined with flat untwisted silk. The fabric is very light and soft to the touch.

Blonde. A silk bobbin lace with large bold flowered design and a delicate mesh ground. There are very good machine-copies of both this and Chantilly.

44

4

DESIGN IN LACE

BEFORE 1800

The word "design" covers three aspects of lace; the stitches used, the purpose for which the piece was shaped and the actual pattern from which it was worked.

Although the first two considerably affect the appearance of each individual piece, it is the wonderful variety and inventiveness of the patterns which contribute most to the fascination of lace design.

The two kinds of lace in which design and craftsmanship rose to the greatest heights were bobbin lace and needlepoint. These two types of work, at first so entirely different in appearance, through being used in similar fashion for trimmings, became more and more alike to look at and eventually conformed so much to the same designs that it became difficult to tell them apart without close inspection. In certain localities, however, and for special purposes, such as ecclesiastical use, individual methods of construction and favourite designs were used, and this can help with identification.

The laces used up to the end of the 16th century were narrow with serrated edges and simple, repetitive, geometrical patterns. Gradually these became a little wider and the designs more ambitious. The points at the edge broadened into scallops and such emblems as the Tudor Rose with sprigs of leaves appeared.

This was the beginning of a tremendous spurt in

technical skill, which, by the middle of the 17th century, achieved a height of beauty and perfection which was never surpassed in the great age of lace-making, and which was to last for another hundred and fifty years. Books of lace patterns of the simpler sort had existed since the 15th century, and had been copied on parchment or widely spread by the use of samplers, but now the services of the finest designers from France, Italy and the Low Countries were called upon.

Many of the mid-17th century designs, particularly those of the highly-priced Gros-Point de Venise, are similar to the flowering scrolls and composite leaves and flowers seen in the beautiful silk brocades of the period, but such was the skill of the workers that they were able to reproduce

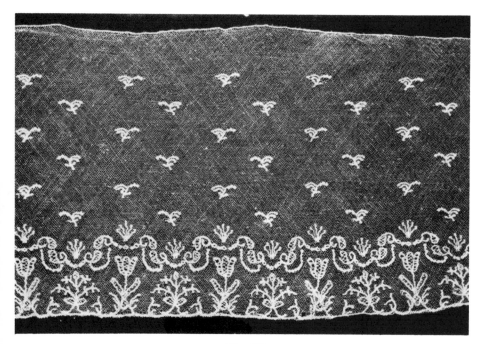

Fig. 26
Lille bobbin lace, showing tulips. Late 18th century. Width: 8½ inches.

46

in an almost three-dimensional effect any design the artist or patron required. Smaller pieces, such as collars, flounces, caps, lappets and rosettes for shoes portrayed flowers of all

Fig. 27
Milanese bobbin lace, showing pot of lilies and pomegranates.
First half of 18th century. Width: 10 inches.

kinds in conventionalised forms—lilies, roses, carnations and fruit blossom. Tulips were often depicted in lace made at Lille. This was a lace much favoured in Holland, being woven with a specially light mesh suitable for use in the caps and ruffles of the national costume. The inclusion of the Dutch national flower was particularly popular *(see Fig. 26)*.

Very large and elaborate pieces were also made. At first these were mainly for church use, as vestments or altar-cloths, and the designs include figures, birds, animals

47

and every possible device of scriptural significance such as the pomegranate, symbol of eternity, and a pot of lilies, symbol of the Annunciation *(see Fig. 27)*. Sometimes they also showed the armorial bearings of the great prelate to whose use the work was dedicated or by whom it was commissioned.

It was not long before the great nobles of European courts followed this example and wonderful panels of lace were made to celebrate events such as royal marriages. The devices and ornaments used for such occasions complimented the recipient, in the fashion of the times, with hunting-scenes, suns and moons in their glory, ministering cherubs, entwined cyphers and anything else which could have a personal application, all bordered and enhanced with floral garlands. Had the pieces been less skilfully designed and less wonderfully worked, their vulgarity would have been appalling, but the effect is only of enchantment at the imagination and skill of another age.

Something should here be said of English laces. Skilled though English workers had always been with embroidery, the refinements of lace-making were learnt mainly through the immigration of refugees from the religious persecutions in European countries, and they never quite rivalled the best achievements of French, Italian and Flemish schools. Though many of the patterns were reproduced with finest workmanship there is a certain awkwardness combined with an interesting individuality.

Patterns which were too frequently used for bobbin lace became, in time, distorted by the prickings of the many pins required for working, and consequently less exact.

In the middle of the 17th century, when panels and caskets were decorated with historical and biblical scenes in padded embroidery, these were also made from needlepoint lace, using an infinite variety of stitches to produce the necessary raised effect. Fine edgings and insertions were also made with the same traditional stitches, sometimes with the date and initials of the worker or the recipient included.

One of the finest of needle laces was Hollie (or holy) point. It was used for christenings or other religious ceremonies, so the designs included such devices as The Tree of Knowledge and Adam and Eve. After the Reformation it was adopted for secular use and being firm and hard-wearing was particularly suitable as an insertion in the backs of babies' caps and the seams of their linen shirts.

During most of the 18th century the quality of lace remained superb, but as increasing quantity was demanded designs tended to become less ambitious and to conform more to a general type of floral spray with elaborate motifs and scrolls to set off the variety of fine, open fillings. All European laces followed much the same fashion but the Italian and French laces tended to favour a curving, more or less continuous, line, while the Flemish designs spread outwards from a central motif. The scalloped edges grew gradually less pronounced, but few of the 18th century laces, with the exception of Lille, have a straight edge. The innumerable beautiful stitches used for the background and to enhance the design deserve to be looked at through a magnifying glass, each being a design in itself. *(See Fig. 17.)*

19TH CENTURY ONWARD

In 1789 the Revolution in France caused such disruption to the lace industry, and such changes in fashion, that there was almost a generation gap before lace again came to be used in any quantity for personal adornment.

During the Regency period, the only lace used for trimming the narrow, flimsy, muslin dresses then in vogue needed to be narrow and light in weight and followed the taste for modish simplicity. The edges of such 19th century lace were straight, bordered with small, stiff flowers and the clear mesh background was varied with little leaves or dots. The laces most favoured at this period were Mechlin, Lille and the types of lace made in the English Midlands, notably Buckinghamshire, the style and meshes of which derived from that of the more expensive imported Flemish laces.

Fig. 28
Christening apron of Isle of Wight Tambour. Early Victorian.

It was not until about 1830 that women's dresses began to be more sumptuous and elaborate, increasing in volume and trimmings to the enormous crinolines of the mid-century. In spite of all the changes of fashion throughout Queen Victoria's reign, women's apparel continued to be heavily trimmed. Naturally the quality of the lace used tended to give way to quantity.

In considering the design of 19th century laces, the most important factor is the invention in the early years of the century of machine-made net. From then on all larger pieces of lace tended to be made from sprigs of bobbin or needle-lace, made separately and applied by hand on to a net background of whatever size and shape fashion decreed. The elimination of the expensive and laboriously hand-made grounds gave a tremendous boost to this type of work and vast lengths of deep flounce and large shawls and fichus were produced in enormous quantities.

The designs applied to net were of elegant floral garlands and sprays with bows and arabesques. The Brussels designs tended to be over-elaborate, the somewhat similar Honiton ones being rather simpler, and incorporating familiar garden and wild flowers. The dress made for the coronation of Queen Adelaide in 1830 was bordered with flowers the initials of which spelt out her name. Work done in Ireland, mainly in convents, by appliqué and tambour embroidery, followed the same trend, with the incorporation of its own emblems of shamrock and even the harp. In the 70's and 80's ferns were very popular for garden and house decoration and often appear in lace design.

Other forms of bobbin and needle-lace making still continued, as well as the sprays used for appliqué, but the edgings of entirely hand-made lace were usually narrow, chiefly for trimming cap-frills and baby-clothes, seldom more than four inches deep, and designs tended to deteriorate. To avoid the tedium of making the mesh ground much lace was made by joining separate sprigs by bobbin or needle-made bridges, and though much of the guipure made in this way is very fine and handsome, by about 1860 the patterns were much debased, particularly in Honiton lace. The original form was often quite lost and the flowers and leaves barely recognisable. The late John Jacoby, an eminent collector, referred in one of his lectures to: "That melancholy soup of assembled motifs which has brought Honiton into disfavour". Silk and cotton bobbin lace was made in Malta and usually incorporates the Maltese Cross, but the designs were mechanical and unimaginative. The industry still continues with the traditional patterns. Needlepoint lace made in Belgium during the 1914 War can often be identified by the use of patriotic motifs *(see Fig. 3)*.

Most Victorian ladies possessed and appreciated the beautiful laces of earlier centuries, and many were distressed by the general deterioration in the industry, caused not only by the availability of good machine-copies but also by better paid work reducing the number of lace-makers. Groups of artistic ladies, not only in England and Ireland but also abroad, made great efforts to re-educate the remaining workers with new designs and to set up a higher standard of both work and pay, but their efforts stood little chance against the current of industrialisation and after the beginning of the 20th century pieces of distinguished quality have only rarely been made.

5

MACHINE LACE

Early in the 19th century, the advance in making net by machine led to experiments in constructing a machine for making lace itself. From about 1830 lace was made by this means and the old patterns were so skilfully reproduced on the machine invented by John Leavers of Nottingham that it takes considerable experience to tell the hand-made from the machine copy.

Most machine laces are made on a loom involving warp and weft, but they cannot truly imitate the twisting and plaiting of bobbins. The réseau of hand-made bobbin lace can be seen twisted into a neat mesh. In machine lace there is often an impression of rigidity of warp and weft. Certain threads pursue a straight direction along the length, pulled together at intervals by a tie thread which gives a tangled look. The same warp and weft look is often noticeable in the toile. In hand-made lace the threads can alter in direction sometimes following the shape of the pattern, whereas machine laces show a tendency for the threads to lie exactly in the direction of the lace and the crossweave to lie at right angles. Sometimes the lengthwise thread appears thicker than the cross thread. It is helpful to remember that machine laces are always made of cotton or synthetic fibre, whereas all old hand-made laces were of flax or silk. Old laces were made with threads not longer than twenty inches due to the limitations of hand spinning, and the joins can sometimes be seen. The threads were, of course, joined before being wound on to the bobbins *(see Fig. 33)*.

Fig. 29
Mechlin bobbin lace, mid-18th century. Machine-made above,
hand-made below.

Valenciennes and Torchon laces are the most difficult to identify. Torchon is made on a different machine, which more closely imitates the movement of the bobbins. Valenciennes is one of the simplest of laces and therefore the easiest to copy successfully. It can be detected by the regularity in the weave and the recurrent errors. Venetian needlepoint and other guipures are imitated by a different process. The design is machine-embroidered on a viscose-type fabric which is later chemically dissolved, leaving the motifs intact and joined only by bridges. In hand-made needlepoint the edges are firmly oversewn with buttonhole stitch. The machine imitation is rough at the edges and the bridges have a crinkly, undefined finish *(see Fig. 34)*. Although machine guipures are often very handsome there is something about their regularity and the frequency of the

Fig. 30
Brussels bobbin appliqué, c. 1860. Machine-made above,
hand-made below.

Fig. 31
Alençon needlepoint, second half of 18th century. Machine-made
above, hand-made below.

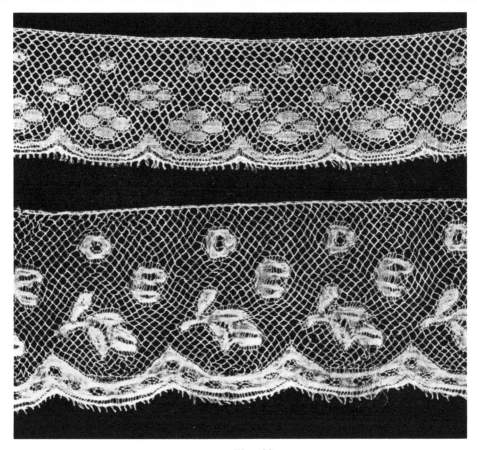

Fig. 32
Valenciennes bobbin, mid-19th century. Machine-made above,
hand-made below.

"repeat" which is less pleasing to the eye than the more imaginative hand-made pieces, and the cotton or synthetic fibres used are harsher to the touch than the older linen thread.

Tambour is chain-stitched by machine on net. The difference is hard to define, other than by a too-frequent regularity and lack of variety in design and working, or by the finish of the back, which may show the action of the machine. The same is true of other machine-embroideries. Neither Carrickmacross nor crochet are likely to be copied by machine.

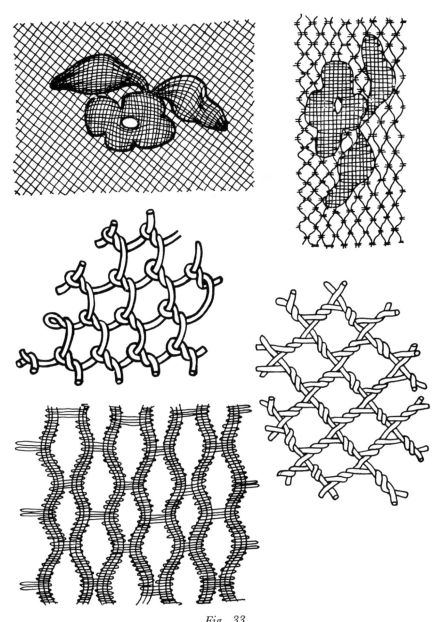

Fig. 33
*(Top to bottom) Left: Bobbin lace. Needleground. Machine
ground. Right: Machine imitation bobbin lace. Bobbin ground.*

It is important to bear in mind that very good machine lace was made well over one hundred years ago. The fact that it "belonged to great-grandma" and has been in the family possession for several generations is no guarantee that it was made by hand.

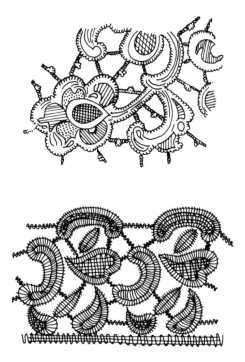

Fig. 34
(Top and bottom) Needlepoint guipure. Machine imitation.

6

DATING LACE

To determine the age of lace needs considerable experience and can seldom be done very exactly. It is not often that lace in a family collection is much older than a hundred years, with the possible exceptions of bridal wear and christening robes. These were put carefully away between use and not subject to ordinary wear and tear like other pieces which were so much used that they often literally wore out.

During the Regency period, when simple nets and muslins were worn, much of the elaborate lace of the previous century and still earlier was thrown away as unfashionable and unusable, exactly as has happened in this century. The pieces that remain from the 18th century can be distinguished by the fineness of design, workmanship and texture. They are often frail and show signs of damage where they have been sewn and unpicked. Generally speaking, the finer the thread and the more intricate the design the older the piece. 17th and 18th century pieces usually have scalloped edges, the deeper the scallop the earlier the piece. Early 19th century laces have straight edges. Early pieces also have a longer "repeat" of the design, even up to fifteen inches.

It must be remembered that both in Brussels and Venice the art of making really fine lace was revived during the second half of the last century, and some of the lace made in these centres at that time is indistinguishable from the earlier pieces except by its newer condition and by the fashion it was made to suit. Before the invention of machine net facilitated the making of large, specially shaped pieces, most lace, with the exception of head-dresses, collars and sleeve-flounces, was made by the piece and adapted to use as required. "Berthas", or shoulder flounces, and full under-sleeves, for instance, are mid-Victorian *(see Fig. 35)*. Narrow lace with a straight edge and a pattern of small dots or sprigs was popular in the early part of the last century. Dating of 19th century lace is greatly helped by reference

Fig. 35
Bertha collar of Brussels mixed lace, c. 1860.

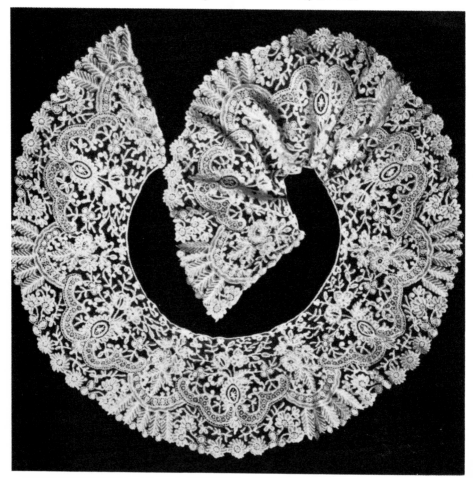

to books on costume, as shawls, caps, collars and cuffs, fans and parasols were also made to meet the requirements of fashion.

Machine-made net was much used as a background for bobbin and needle sprays, sewn on by hand. Honiton and Brussels wedding veils and flounces made in this way may be anything up to a hundred and thirty years old, although as the patterns and styles of these changed very little, their age can only be guessed by comparative fineness or established by family tradition. Small apron-shaped or semi-circular veils were either christening veils or were worn with a bonnet, an early Victorian fashion. Much of the beautifully embroidered cambric used for babies' gowns, with open needle-lace worked into the flowers, dates from the middle of the 19th century and was made in Ayrshire and was sometimes called "Scotch hole". The older dresses were very long and had adjustable, open, necks and waists, with short frills over the shoulders. Dresses heavily trimmed with lace and insertion were late 19th century, and the lace was usually machine-made. If the sleeves are long the dress is probably dated between 1895 and 1910. By the end of the century the traditional lace patterns had become large and coarse and were generally joined by bridges rather than by hand-made réseau or by applying to net. Flounces and edgings, which in earlier times had been made fifteen inches wide or even more, tended to become narrower, as the wider pieces were too costly and could be made much more cheaply by machine. The designs gradually deteriorated.

Most Irish laces date from the middle of the 19th century and some are still being made. The different types of embroidery on net are exquisite work and the best pieces are likely to be from seventy to a hundred years old. The typical Irish crochet, worked from a central flower, was not a very early development. As it is strong and durable and has not changed in style, it is not possible to date, except by the fashion it was made to suit, such as caps and collars. Crochet made in imitation of needlepoint was an earlier form of lace and might be over a hundred years old *(Figs. 21, 22)*.

Lace handkerchiefs (*see Figs. 19, 20*) can very often be dated by their size. In the 1840's it was fashionable to carry a handkerchief instead of a fan. These measured as much as twenty-five inches square, but became gradually smaller during the next hundred years. A handkerchief made in 1850 measures nineteen inches square, and one made in 1870 fourteen inches square, whereas those made about 1930 measure no more than eight inches. They are trimmed with a variety of lace and embroidery and can make an interesting collection by themselves. Although lace handkerchiefs were certainly used as far back as the reign of Queen Elizabeth I, very few survive which are more than a hundred and thirty years old.

7

CLEANING AND REPAIRING

Lace which has been put away for many years is often dirty, stained and even torn. Its beauty cannot be appreciated until it has been restored as far as possible to its original condition.

Lace is much stronger than its appearance would suggest, and will generally stand up quite well to washing and mild bleaching and starching, although silk lace, such as Maltese, does not wash well. Carrickmacross is also not easy to treat in this manner successfully, owing to shrinkage. If the lace is really rotten it is best, however old and interesting the piece may be, to throw it away. If it has become frail through age and use, it is wiser not to treat it unless the condition is so filthy as to be wholly unacceptable. If it must be washed, tack it carefully to a piece of linen first. Often one finds that the cambric of a handkerchief has perished but the lace surround is still sound; then the handkerchief can be recentred with a piece of fine cambric or a very soft plain handkerchief. A dirty piece should first be left to soak in cold water for at least an hour. Then make a solution of pure soap flakes in a saucepan nearly full of lukewarm water. Put in the rinsed lace and bring it slowly to the boil, keeping it simmering for about ten minutes, controlling it with a wooden spoon. Lift it carefully into a large bowl of soft water and rinse well, pulling the fabric as little as possible. Remove it and squeeze it out in a clean cloth. Then examine each piece for discoloration.

Almost all old lace will show brownish spots. Stains on silk lace cannot be removed, but white cotton or flax lace can be much improved by the use of ordinary household bleach. Make up the weakest solution recommended on the label and, having spread the damp lace on a clean white cloth, gently dab the stains with a piece of cotton wool soaked in the solution. Continue to dab at intervals for about half an hour until the stains are almost invisible, then rinse the treated part well and continue on further stains in the same way. Some black or greenish mould stains will react to hydrogen peroxide. Discoloration on black lace should be dabbed with vinegar.

Sometimes pieces of lace based on net are very limp. If they are to be used, it freshens them to treat them with a very weak solution of starch. If the lace washes whiter than is desired, it can be tinted by steeping in weak cold tea to which a few drops of ink should be added. Iron the lace over a soft cloth while it is still damp, using a cool iron. Where there is a raised pattern it should be placed downwards.

Lace with a net ground is almost impossible to repair invisibly, but small holes and rents in the design can be much improved by careful mending or by sewing a small piece of pattern over the hole. Guipures, such as Honiton, with motifs joined by bridges (see Fig. 9), can be pinned to a firm cushion and the bridges remade in fine chain or button-hole stitch. Fine thread is not easy to come by, but some can be unwound from old bobbins. Any good piece of lace is worth some trouble, if only for the pleasure of seeing something which looked like a grubby rag restored to its original beauty.

8

USING AND STORING

Some pieces of lace, such as veils, trains, flounces and even collars and cuffs, can occasionally be used to meet the demand of modern fashion but, in general, lace is not often worn.

Large pieces of wide flounce, both black and white, can be made into beautiful dresses, but it is difficult to decide whether it is right to cut them, and it must be remembered that they will not stand up to hard wear. It would be a pity to spoil a very old and rare piece by using it, but Honiton, Limerick and Carrickmacross are still comparatively plentiful. Damaged pieces and oddments can be made into christening robes or simple baby dresses *(see Fig. 36)*. By skilful mounting and joining small scraps can be turned into delightful table sets or covers for small cushions *(see Fig. 37)*. Handkerchiefs, which have been recentred, can be used. Sometimes they are sufficiently decorative to frame, singly or in twos and threes, partly superimposed, on a coloured mount. Any piece which is of considerable age, or complete in itself, should not be cut or altered unnecessarily, but when one thinks of the hours, months, even years, spent on making a length of lace, surely the maker would prefer it to be used and enjoyed, even briefly, rather than to be stored away and never looked at, touched, or enjoyed again.

However, most laces, like many other collections, must be stored. This should be done in such a way that they can be produced for inspection looking their best.

Fig. 36
Christening robe made from a damaged veil of mid-Victorian
Brussels needlepoint appliqué.

Fig. 37
Cushion covers made from lace scraps.

Handkerchiefs should not be folded, but rolled in a piece of material wider than the largest and half as long again. One end of this should have a padded roll along it, and the other ribbons for tying. The handkerchiefs should be separated by different-coloured pieces of tissue paper *(see Fig. 38)*. Narrow edgings can be mounted on a somewhat similar folder. Choose a soft, bright material two yards long. One third should be folded inwards lengthwise, sewn up at the ends and tacked across at about eight inch intervals. The pieces of lace are then tacked across the

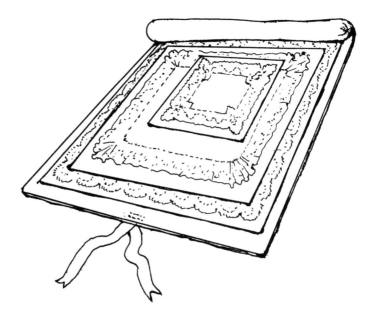

Fig. 38
Handkerchiefs stored for display.

inner fold, any surplus length being tucked inside *(see Fig. 39)*. Collars can also be tacked to the single fold. This sampler should be folded over and over to a small size and tied or buttoned. Larger pieces should be carefully folded with a piece of coloured tissue immediately under the top fold so that the beauty of the design can be seen. These can be kept in boxes or plastic bags and take up very little room. The best containers are antique needlework or cutlery boxes, and it is surprising how much they will hold. Small scraps of special interest may conveniently be kept in photograph albums with "slip-in" transparent leaves.

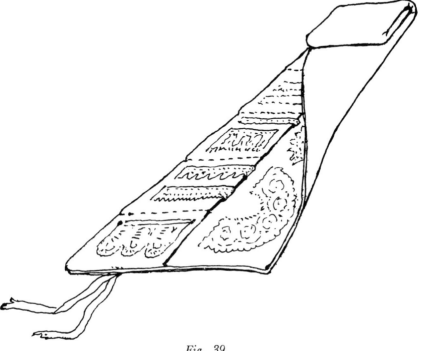

Fig. 39
Lace edging stored for display.

THE VALUE OF LACE

There are many products of craftsmanship, cheap and little thought of at the time they were made, which now, on account of fashion or rarity, have a very high value. The interesting thing about antique lace is that during the many centuries that it was made up until the beginning of this century it was highly appreciated both in terms of beauty and money. Now, nearly seventy years later, it has almost no market value at all. There is certainly no other craft of which this can be said.

The value of a collection of lace is therefore a purely personal one and depends mainly on individual bargaining between buyer and seller. Such things as fans and parasols have collectable value in themselves and there is occasional demand for lace wedding-veils which can be bought for somewhere between £50 and £100 in this country, according to quality and condition. In America they are much more highly priced, as is all antique lace.

Collars and cuffs, scarves, shawls and other Victorian costume pieces are plentiful and still fetch very low prices, from a few pence to a few pounds, as do 19th century lengths of flounce, even in good condition.

On the other hand, all lace of the 18th century and earlier, even if it is in poor condition, is much sought after by collectors. Cap-backs and lappets may fetch from £15 to £40 at auction, and good pieces of flounce from £3 to £10 a yard. Hollie-point is especially rare and desirable and fairly extensively collected.

Lace no longer holds any place in the world of fashion, but it is difficult to believe that, on account simply of its age and inherent beauty, it will not one day be better appreciated in the world of antiques.

GLOSSARY OF TERMS

APPLIQUÉ	Lace or fine cambric on machine net.
BARS	Used instead of réseau to connect the toile.
BERTHA	Flounce shaped to wear round shoulders.
BOBBIN LACE	Made from threads attached to bobbins.
BOBBINS	Small elongated wooden or bone reels on which the thread is wound.
BRIDES/BRIDGES	See "Bars".
CORDONNET	Heavier thread used to outline pattern.
CUTWORK	Embroidery with background cut away.
DARNED NET	Embroidery on machine net.
DUCHESSE	A mixed lace.
FILET	Pattern on hand-made square mesh.
FILLINGS	Different types of stitches.
FOOTINGS	Narrow edge sewn to the straight side of flounces to strengthen them.
GAZE	Gauze, a form of needle ground.
GROUND	Woven background.
GUIPURE	Lace of bold design with joining bars or open ground.
LACIS	See "Filet".
LAPPETS	Decorative pieces hanging from the sides of a head-dress.
MESH	See "Ground".
NEEDLEPOINT	Lace made with needle and thread in buttonhole stitch.
PICOTS	Tiny loops.
POINT	Term loosely applied to fine quality lace.

RESÉAU	See "Ground".
RETICELLA	Early form of needle lace.
SAMPLER	Examples of lace mounted for display.
TAMBOUR	Worked on machine net with a fine hook.
TOILE	The solid part of a design.